THE LOVE OF
RABIACCA

TEACHINGS OF
THE ORDER OF CHRISTIAN MYSTICS

THE LOVE OF RABIACCA

Teachings of The Order of Christian Mystics

The "Curtiss Books" freely available at

www.orderofchristianmystics.co.za

THE LOVE OF RABIACCA

A TRAGEDY IN FIVE ACTS

A Tale of a Prehistoric Race
Recovered Psychically

By Dr. and Mrs. Frank Homer Curtiss
Founders of The Order of Christian Mystics

2015 EDITION

REPUBLISHED FOR THE ORDER BY
MOUNT LINDEN PUBLISHING
JOHANNESBURG, SOUTH AFRICA
ISBN: 978-1-920483-26-5

"Ministers of Christ and Stewards of the Mysteries of God."
1 Corinthians 4 vs. 1

PREFACE

Having read of the wonderful psychic power of concentrated thought, a small company of friends decided to experiment with it. Mrs. C, being the most sensitive member of the party, was selected as the subject of the experiment.

With the light turned low Mrs. C. lay down upon a couch, while the others formed a circle around her and crooned a soft melody. Soon a slight spasmodic twitching of Mrs. C. showed that she had contacted super-physical forces. Her hand was gradually raised and remained fixed.

The authors, in trying to replace the arm, discovered to their amazement that her whole body had become rigid and that she was pointing in horror to a sight presented to her inner vision. Soon she began to talk, and calling each of the party by strange names, she described and seemed actually to experience and to live the events related.

From notes taken at the time, the authors have arranged the following short narrative of the events as they were described, and those present at the time have since vouched for their accuracy.

Mrs. C. is not a subjective medium nor a spiritualist, and at no time did she pass into a state of trance, but retained her consciousness throughout the experience.

CONTENTS

ACT I

THE BATTLEMENTS

"SO AT last thou art come, my lord, Zanzibaris! When yonder moon had stretched its shadows across the court below, and thou wert not here, I feared that my lord had forgotten his promise to give me this last hour's speech with him alone."

"And how should a soldier not keep his word with Princess Maldingo?" replied the warrior.

Princess Maldingo was of the royal house of Quetzacoatl, and the King's brother, Prince Zanzibaris, had but just returned from his triumphal campaigns against the tribes of the farther provinces to attend the burial ceremonies of his brother, the dead King. They stood on a small battlement of the palace overlooking the city. To their left and behind them rose the nearby mountains, whose snow-capped peaks lay enveloped in rolling masses of blackened clouds. To their right lay Lake Tulare with its famous Chinampas or floating islands on which were grown the luscious fruits and vegetables for the King's table, and the flowers for the ceremonial decoration of the temples. Beyond the lake stretched out the fertile valley of Tolotlan with its irrigating ditches marking off the silvery lines of the cultivated fields into little patches of green and gold. At their feet lay the city of Iztamal, slumbering and silent, save for the pacing of the solitary sentinels on its massive walls, and the occasional late arrival of delegations from the subject cities coming to be present at the King's obsequies.

The slowly creeping clouds had already half veiled the light which the full moon shed in tropical splendor o'er the many stately palaces and the majestic Temple of the Sun which made the city famous throughout the then known world.

"I have but just come from assigning our barbarian chieftains to their camping places without the city wall," said Zanzibaris.

"I had thought perhaps a more tender duty had made thee tardy to this tryst," replied the Princess.

"Thou speakest, I know, of Rabiacca, and indeed I am but a short time come from her."

"'Twas not to speak of our Queen's waiting woman but of the Queen herself that I asked thee here this hour."

"What more hast thou learned of her?"

"The priests and wise men and the Council of the Twenty Lords have met in final conclave this day, and on the morrow will decree that, despite the laws of our founderking, Iztamna, and despite the ancient custom of our race, the White Queen shall not ascend the Flaming Pyre, and in that holy flame meet the glorious fate of going with her lord and serving him in the strange lands of the gods."

"Most wisely have they spoken, for as thou knowest well, our Queen, Tishana, is far more than mortal, and were she to leave us now, how then could our priests speak with the gods and how could the gods impart their instructions to our men of learning?"

"'Twas ever thus with warriors to believe the guidance of the gods achieved the victories their own prowess won. Thou hast been absent, yes these fifteen years, save to attend the seven-year festivals, and thou knowest her but little, and doth believe all the strange tales that are told concerning her. I who, as a foster sister, have lived with her here within these palace walls, do know her life full well. Ever since the day, when but a girl, she was found wandering on our mountain side and was brought thence to our loved King, I have studied her, and I do know she is but mortal as are ourselves."

"But did she not come from the Land-Beyond-the-Mountains where no mortal has ever trod; where wise men say dwell all the gods? And was ever one, among the darkskinned races of our world, like unto her?"

"Too well I know how the sight of her white skin and yellow hair, with her great blue eyes and strange-sounding voice, did charm and cause to turn me from our departed King. But I tell thee that 'twas by magic she did do these things!"

"How may that be when she communes with the very highest gods upon the sacred mountain and brings their inspiration to our priests and men of learning?"

"Can it be that thou, a warrior and a leader of our race, can yet be blinded by such things? And because at sight of her thy elder brother, for full five days, could eat no meat nor be amused by dancing girls nor music of the reeds, for love of her, wilt thou too, then, give up the kingdom that, by right, should fall to thee, and permit her to live and reign here still as Queen? Wilt thou leave thy brother companionless and alone in the lands of the gods? And all in violation of the sacred Ceremony of the Flaming Pyre?"

"Yet, if she should join the King, my brother, according to the custom, how then could the gods teach us the wisdom that, since her coming, hath raised our people to be rulers of the world, and brought success to every venture of our arms and to every art and knowledge our men of learning have yet put forth?"

"Thinkest thou that the gods will still send their blessing on a thing usurped or on the usurper? And am not I, Princess Maldingo, famed as a mighty sorceress?"

"But well 'tis known that the powers evoked by thee art called unholy, and were only turned to useful ends by the divine gift of our White Priestess-Queen."

"Even so 'tis said by them that envy my power. But thinkest thou not that with thee on thy rightful throne and with me at thy side as Priestess-Queen, the gods would withhold from me aught that they have given her? Tis our race they love, not this fair-skinned foreigner who comes whence no one knows!"

"But, though thou shouldst persuade me that the throne is mine by right, and that it is our race the gods descend to help, how could thou then be made my Queen, when Rabiacca is my other self, destined by all the stars to be with me one soul?"

"So was she thy other self, and might have been thy soul, had not she herself dissolved the bond by loving in thy stead her foster brother, Mungo, who even now commands the palace guards."

"Thy words recall what I have noticed oft since my return, that she seemed not happy in my presence as of yore, as though oppressed by some dread foreboding that even put its spell on me. This very night she seemed distraught and feverish, as if some tragic ill impended."

"I am glad to see that thou art not so blind as still to cling to the love of a waiting woman, when at thy feet a Princess of the royal blood, aflame with love of thee, pours out her heart and humiliates herself to show it thus. And all that thou mayest be our King as by all the laws and sacred rites thou shouldst be."

"Still, tell me how may it be when long ago Rabiacca was betrothed to me in the temple when we were yet but children. And ere I went to war I bore upon my breast the raw imprint of those dear wounds from which did flow my blood to mingle in the golden bowl with hers, and make us one in blood and soul?"

"Have I not told thee that her unfaithfulness hath snapped the bond and let the twin flame of thy spirit shine in me? Thinkest thou that Princess Maldingo could not love thee then as much as the waiting woman? Are not my arms thus clasped about thy neck as soft as ever hers? Cannot the hotpressed kisses of these royal lips blot out the memory of her timid touch? But see the size and wealth of this dark hair of mine that reaches o'er thy knees so straight and long, and by it judge the warmth my love will bring."

"The saying is that woman's hair, when coarse and long, is but the sign of passion's strength, and not the pure cold flame of that true love which Venus gives to those whom she selects as mates."

"Ah, my dear lord! Cannot the soft warmth of my woman's breast, close pressed against thy heart, melt that cold and priestly prejudice with which thou withholdest me thy love? Nor cause response of one returning throb? Shall not the very excess of the passion that thou speakest of, made pure and quickened by that ray which comes to me down from my planet, the mighty Mars, great ruler of my destiny, cause me to pour out on thee such flood of ecstasy as shall bring to me the answering thrill of love returned?"

"Release thine arms! The perfume of thy breath doth make me faint."

"Turn not from me, love, my lord. I feel the warmth of thy awakened blood flood all thy face and in thy hands burn hot. Ah, thou cold of heart! But let these aching lips seek thine again, so shalt thou know what wealth of love my royal blood can give."

"I cold of heart? Callest thou me cold of heart? More like I am an all-consuming fire. My blood doth course through all my flesh like molten brass white hot and fervent unto death. I cold of heart? When first thy hand reached out to lie in mine upon the parapet, my very bones began to thrill with that wondrous spell thy witchery hath wove. And I forgot all else save the soft roundness of thy woman's form and the piercing blackness of thy fathomless eyes. Quench once more my inward fire in the delirium of thy lips, that I may forget all else but that I love thee, and that to love thee is all bliss."

"An thou lovest me, then wilt thou sware to be my king, and take thy rightful place upon the throne and see the sacred customs of our race fulfilled?"

"So do I sware! Only let me have again thy lips! Ah! . . . But how may I accomplish thy desire? One may not slay the Queen and brave the populace who hold her sacred?"

"That can the power of my magic spells accomplish well, my lord. Nor shalt thou, my love, have aught to do but hold thy sword straight pointed toward her breast, and by the spells that I do chant, thy blade shalt gain a magic power to strike her through the heart."

"It shall be done. Tis all for thee! I am thy slave!"

"Come quickly then. Let our love wait. Twill but the stronger grow. For even now she kneels before the Flame deep in the secret crypt beneath the Sun God's shrine, praying for a maiden who hath sought her aid. Be quick, my lord. Already it is nearing dawn, and the gathering storm seems about to break upon our heads."

ACT II

THE MOUNTAIN SIDE

'THE last lingering note of the sunset bell was dying on the evening breeze. Near a shrine upon the sacred Mountain-of-the-Gods stood the Priestess-Queen, Tishana. Her face was turned toward the setting sun, her arms outstretched, and there was a look of far-off glory in the depths of her great blue eyes. Over her white robe, her yellow hair, illumined by the tints of red and gold, flashed from the sinking sun, enveloped her like a fleecy cloud of shimmering light. Seen at such a moment, well might the people think she had descended from the sun to teach her chosen people how to rule the world, as indeed the priests had said.

As the last lingering beams of light disappeared behind the mountain peaks, the Priestess' lips murmured a farewell prayer to the departing god of day. Dropping her arms, a faint sigh caught her ear, and turning, she beheld her favorite waiting woman and companion, Rabiacca, kneeling at her feet.

"What is it, Rabiacca, my loved sister," she said with a smile of welcome, "that makes thee venture on the sacred mountain past the Stone-of-the-Sun that marks the usual boundaries of approach? Hast thou climbed all this steep path to say farewell with me to glorious Tonathiu?"*

"Nay, nay, my Queen; I come to speak to thee as to a mother whose love divineth all her child's heart hath need to say."

"Speak, sweet sister mine. For thou dost know my love for thee wilt grant thee all the comfort it can give."

"I am so oppressed and sad I could not live within myself another hour, and so I come to thee to bare my heart."

"Sit down upon this mound and pillow here thy head upon my knee—so. Now tell me what it is that troubleth thee."

"'Tis fear for my dear lord, Prince Zanzibaris, that weighs upon my heart. Thou dost know that, when but still a child, I was pledged to him at some mysterious altar whose form I yet recall

_____
* God of the Sun.

deep beneath the temple floor. And when he had reached the age
for war, and had buckled on his maiden sword to go abroad and
win his right to be called a man, he, of his own free will, did renew
in his heart's warm blood his troth to me. And on my body do I
bear a precious scar where the stream of our two bleeding hearts
did mingle—and yet methinks he loves me not. The scar upon my
breast hath festered since his return as if the drops instilled had
slowly nurtured poison.

So sore it is that at those rare times when still he clasps my heart
to his, I tremble and shrink from his embrace. Nor dare I tell him
what I feel. And daily in the Assembly his glance doth ever seek
the eyes of our royal Princess, Maldingo, and I see them burn and
flash and linger there."

At the mention of Zanzibaris' name, the Priestess, Tishana,
gazed far out over the mountains toward the blaze of glory left
by the sunken sun, unseeing. She seemed about to speak, but each
time her lips parted, a spasm of emotion choked back the words;
meanwhile her hands with caressing touch still smoothed aside
the raven strands from Rabiacca's brow. At last, with an effort of
control, she turned her gaze upon the young girl's face, and one
could almost swear that in her eyes were glistening, unshed tears.

"Sweet sister," the Priestess replied, "thou shaft have all my
help.

Full well I know that Zanzibaris doth wish his throne. I, in his
eyes, am but a base usurper, and Maldingo has impressed deep
this thought upon his ambitious soul and pictured to his mind the
greatness of his reign. Ye gods! How gladly could I give it him!
But at this time he could not understand my thought in it. Perhaps
I should ascend the Flaming Pyre of my departed lord—who never
was my rightful lord, the gods declare. He wed me when I was but
a child, and at that time the wise men did favorably cast the circle
of the stars at his command but to save their heads.

"But hush! Thou didst not hear me speak those words! Turn
thou thine innocent eyes away from mine! I cannot bear their gaze.
They seem to search my inmost thoughts. Since now 'tis said,
I'll tell thee that, though I was made his Queen, I never loved my

lord. And so how can I follow then and serve him in those other lands where every heart is read as clearly as the carven symbols on the palace gate?

"But I will help thee, Rabiacca. Tis but thy right to wed with Zanzibaris. And I, the Sun God's bride, will aid thee by my power from on high. No! no!" she half whispers, "no thought of mortal love shall make less clear the depths of my aspiring soul. All the mighty force that I do gain from yonder sinking sun, my Lord, my God, will I exert to foil that sorceress' plot, and bring to thee thy happiness. "Stay thou up on the mountain, child, and I will tell thee what herbs of mystic potency to gather. And when, at midnight, thou hast culled all seven kinds kneel thou upon this rock and pray until morning's dawn doth give thee first its golden rays—then seek me out. And while thou prayest, deep within the temple altar's heart will I perform the sacred Fire Sacrifice; and all the night will feed the holy Flame with magic herbs, and gather from its fiery breath the god's intent. Promise me, 'loved sister, that thou wilt not return 'til morning dawns, nor ever turn thine eyes toward the city gates. Let no inner sense, no augury, distract thy pure soul from its lone midnight vigil. Pray earnestly and come to me at sunrise. And now good night; I leave thee, but fear thou not. Good night, good night."

"But stay, my Queen! Thou art so sad! Indeed I am but cruel, selfish, thus to pour my troubles in thine ears, and on this sad night of all the nights! I had forgot that thou wouldst be all distraught because thy lord goeth hence upon the Flame tomorrow and thou goest not with him. But thou art so strong and noble! This night, methinks, if 'twere my lord that went alone, I would spend in sorrow's thrall, and tears enough I'd shed to bear his soul unto the shores of bliss. To leave him thus alone! Ah me! What is my sorrow unto thine?"

"My child, thou dost not understand. As Queen, well did I serve my lord, the King. But now I owe a duty to my over-lord, even the great god Tonathiu, and he bids me cherish all true love and haste it to its fulfilling. So will I begin with thine this night and bring to fruit thy happiness. Farewell, farewell!"

Sadly, taking the young girl's face between her hands, and looking tenderly into her eyes, the Priestess pressed a lingering kiss upon her lips, then turning, went slowly down the mountain, leaving Rabiacca to gather the herbs with which to make her love philter.

ACT III

THE TEMPLE CRYPT

TURN here, my lord. This is the secret passage from the Priestess' chamber of preparation by which she comes to pray before going to the public service of the temple, and at each midnight hour. Its opening is at the side, behind the pillar of Venus. It is close to the altar, and is not seen from the palace passage nor from that by which the priests descend. There shalt thou, in one full stride, stand close behind her as she kneels before the Flame. And with thy sword straight pointed toward her heart, shall her end come peacefully, and without harm to thee. But be thou careful that thou makest no sound, nor cause her to turn and break my spell."

Closely following Zanzibaris, the Princess Maldingo stepped from the passage into the little round chamber that formed the crypt. This chamber, hewn from the living rock, was necessarily small, not over seven paces in diameter, with a bell-shaped dome some three spans in height at the center. At equal distances around the walls stood twelve pillars of pure, white marble, around each of which there twined a large serpent of solid gold, in whose eyes were set a rose-pink gem. Around a smaller circle within these pillars stood seven others, six of which were each of different colored onyx, and one of pure gold, studded with immense jewels. At the side, opposite the golden pillar, upon a small pyramid reached by seven steps, stood a block of clear, translucent stone resembling crystal, an arm's length in each dimension. A thin, pale flame rose from a bowl-shaped depression cut in its top, and was reflected from a symbol of the sun emblazoned in solid gold upon the center of a great balanced cross of white marble which stood close behind the altar. Just above the cross, apparently floating in the air, was a white swan with outstretched wings, also having jewels for its eyes.

Not a sound broke the solemn stillness of that subterranean chamber save the murmur of the Priestess' voice as she knelt on the topmost step of the altar. From time to time she cast into the

flame certain mystic herbs, whose pungent, aromatic odors seemed
to exalt the higher faculties of her soul to ecstasy. With each herb
she repeated mantram, and with the last, shaking free the folds of
her flowing robe, she raised her arms to the now glowing symbol
of the sun, and half prayed, half chanted the solemn invocation
of the Fire Sacrifice.

"Ascending Flame, within whose all-encircling arms all
substance must be dissolved, all lower forces transmuted into
the all-creating force of Love, let Thy hot breath burn 'round my
trembling soul, and consume all earthly dross. Let Thy purifying
heat transmute into god-like love all my mortal thoughts, that I,
Thy Priestess, may stand on earth Thy virgin bride, unsullied e'en
by a thought of mortal love, as stand those souls who, after many
lives and many funeral burnings, at last attain perfection.

"O Thou great and glorious One! to whom all men turn in time
of need! Thou wondrous embodiment of the all-creative power
that dwelleth in our sun! Accept, we pray, the incense of these
our burnt offerings. And as the potent force of life, imprisoned by
Thee within these herbs, ascends to its divine Creator, so mayest
ascend to Thine embrace the adoration of this humble heart and
the service of this my life.

"As the tongues of flame shrivel up the form and transmute the
substance of these herbs that their soul-force may be set free, so
may the Divine Creative Fire of these two hearts, Thy children
Zanzibaris and Rabiacca, joined by the force of pure mortal love
and watered with the rain of perfect sympathy and due respect,
purge from their minds the dross of earthly passion and flow forth
creative and ennobling unto a future life.

"Accept, we beseech Thee, the sacrifice of all earthly joy in
the person of this, Thy Priestess, and give to them the happiness
of perfect love on earth that through its mystic power they may
evolve to mastery. Accept, O great God of Fire, the body, the
life, the soul of this Thy Priestess, and let her life be even as the
withered herbs, that the divine spark of their united lives may
ever fly straight up to be at one with Thee. Send down Thy swift,

pure ray into their souls, that they may see Thee face to face and worship Thee aright.

"Thus as the warmth and the light and the force of Thy outer breath hath made these herbs to grow and bloom, so may Thy inner breath perfect and bring to birth their inner selves. Seven times, O Glorious One, did I cast into the Flame the seven herbs of power. Three times doth Thy Priestess prostrate herself before Thine altar that Thou mayest accept the living sacrifice so freely made that Love may reign supreme."

Scarce had she finished the three prostrations when Maldingo, fearing that this solemn scene would unnerve the Prince for the crime she had planned for him, coughed harshly. And as the Priestess, startled, turned half toward the outstretched blade, Maldingo clutched the Prince's arm and fiercely whispered, "Strike!" With his senses still enmeshed in the spell of passion, uncomprehending the Priestess' words, and with Maldingo's hot whisper in his ear, scarce knowing what he did, he thrust the sword straight through the Priestess' breast. With a smothered cry of "Oh! Thou? My Lord?" she fell upon the upper steps, clutching at the sculptured figures on the altar's side. Even as the thrust was made, a frenzied cry of "Hold! In the name of great Teotl!" rang out from the farther side of the chamber. And in a few quick bounds the pale and frantic priest, Balixus, stood before them.

"Thou! Zanzibaris? Thou, my brother? Thou the murderer of our Priestess-Queen? What baleful mystery is this, that such a crime can dye thy hands with sacred blood and stain thy soul throughout the ages hence? Who is that with thee there, that shrinking seeks to hide behind thy cloak? Ah, thou, then, that with thy unholy spells hast brought my brother to this foul deed! Well know I now the meaning of the portent that our Queen these many days hath had, of evil deeds impending!"

The priest, kneeling beside the fallen Queen, raises her stricken form gently in his arms and finds the flow of blood already stopped. Zanzibaris, pale and shaken, stands transfixed with horror. Cold beads of perspiration gather on his brow, and his eyes stare wide and fascinated at the fallen Priestess' face.

What cord of mystery did that dying look awake? What memories of a dim and misty past swept o'er his soul? Suddenly, with a half stifled moan, he realizes what the last words of the Priestess had revealed. At last he sees that he has been but the tool of the designing and heartless Princess Maldingo.

Mistaking his silence, Maldingo says, "Tis well deserved, this death, to one who would set at naught our sacred rites, and seize our kingdom, and usurp thy lawful throne, my Prince."

"Silence, woman! or witch, or whatever kind of female thing thou art, that evil spirits use to work their damning deeds! Freed now thy passion's spell, too well I see what desire of thine own advance hath worked in thee to plan this awful deed of mine. And I, weak fool, to listen to thy siren words, and thus, in one fell act, foresware all love and bring to death the Priestess of our people, through whom alone the gods gave greatness to our race."

The priest Balixus, rising then, speaks. "Should any leave this scene alive, how might we then explain our Priestess death without delivering thee, my brother, to slow torture's rack? There is but one thing left to do when in the noble line injustice irreparable has been wrought, and that, the 'Rite of the Naked Sword.'"

"And gladly do I welcome it," the Prince replied, "that I may follow her, and by my sacrifice and faithful service in those other lands in which she wanders strive, through ages hence, to undo the wrong I did this day, and return to her the goddess love she bore for me. Make us thy priestly oath, my brother, and we will swear it fast." The priest then took the bloody sword that Zanzibaris had dropped and holding it out toward his brother, said, "Take then this sword dipped in thy Priestess' martyred blood, and make the sacred cross upon the woman too. Now, swear by the ancient 'Rite of Naked Sword' that was ordained since first our race began; and by the sacred threefold ray of our most high god Tolque-Nahuaque, that in all thy future lives, through all the lands that thou shalt wander, and whate'er thy many changing state, thou wilt seek out our Priestess-Queen and serve her with thy life's best blood, until such ages hence have passed as shall atone to her the wrong that thou hast this day done."

"By the ancient 'Rite of Naked Sword,' and by the threefold ray of our most high god Tolque-Nahuaque, I so do swear to serve her with my life's best blood, until the debt is wholly paid, and I restore to her the love she sacrificed for me this night".

Maldingo sinks down upon the cold stone floor and, covering her face with her hands, moans distractedly.

"Swear, woman!" thundered the Prince. "Why clingest thy ready tongue so dry to thy fear-shrunk lips? Swear, I say! Swear!" Maldingo, with a terrified look murmurs through her blanched lips, "I swear."

Then they cast lots to see who first shall plunge upon the upright sword. The first lot falls to the priest, Balixus. Turning to the Prince, his brother, he says, "Farewell, dear brother. As I have kept faithful watch over our loved Queen here, so shall I ever watch o'er her in times to come, and remind thee of thy oath. Be thou faithful unto it. Farewell!"

As he falls upon the sword, Maldingo groans and shudders, for unto her the second lot has fallen. Turning imploringly to the Prince she pleads: "Ah, force me not, good Zanzibaris, to do this awful thing! I do not want to die! Twas not I that did the deed, but thou! And though I counseled it, 'twas but for thine own good and prompted by my love for thee."

"Fulfill thy oath! Nor speak to me of thy unholy love in this dread vault of death. Thy turn! Be quick!"

"Ah! but do let me live a day and I will pray for thee a thousand prayers before the Sun God's shrine."

"Clasp so the sword—so. What! Must I then hold thy coward hand upon the hilt? Now! Whilst I grip fast thy trembling hand, one plunge and then I'll follow thee."

The Prince forces her to fall upon the sword while he holds her hand upon the hilt and steadies it. He then places the sword against his own breast and falls upon it, across the bodies of the other two, at the foot of the altar.

ACT IV

THE LOVE PHILTER

RABIACCA, left alone up on the mountain side, began at once to gather the herbs indicated by the Priestess. It was no easy task to pick them in the exact manner prescribed and to remember the proper mantram that must be said as each flower was plucked. And thus for a while, she was so intent upon her task that she took no heed of the muttering storm that was creeping down the mountain side. On and on she wandered until she had gathered all but one herb, the last and most potent. The Priestess had told her that this last flower stood for the last letter of the Sacred Word without which the charm would be of no avail. And since, if it were gathered in the shadow, its portent would be dark, Rabiacca prayed most earnestly for just one more ray of moonlight that the philter might be perfect. But the rapidly descending clouds had now completely obscured the face of the moon. Rabiacca, not daring to turn homeward toward the city, stumbled on, trembling with fear both that she would fail in her important task and of the approaching storm. At last her groping hand touched an immense rock, one of the "Stones-of-the-Sun" standing upright in her path. Despairing further search, and kneeling with her outstretched arms in the form of a cross, she prayed, "O Mother Meztli,* give me light! But one faint ray from Thy dear face that I may find the flower that shall win my lord. In the holy name of Love do I implore Thee grant my prayer."

The words were scarce uttered when a blinding flash, accompanied by a terrific peal of thunder, struck the rock before which she knelt and split it from top to bottom. In the instant of time before unconsciousness came she distinctly saw the flower she desired growing in a crevice of the rock. Was it only a trick of her failing senses or did she really see? The flower seemed to be blooming upon the top of a burning funeral pyre. How clearly she could see the flames curl and rise around it; and yet the little

---
* Goddess of the Moon.

flower lifted up its head unharmed. And just above it, as if floating in the flame itself, she seemed to see the forms of Zanzibaris and the Priestess clasped in each other's arms. Each face bore a look of glad triumph which changed to an expression of tender love as they turned their eyes toward her and reached out their arms. Rabiacca held out her hand and tried to reach them and the little flower, but she could not accomplish this without ascending the burning pyre itself. Oh, surely, surely had her prayer been answered! Not only Meztli but great Izcozauhqui himself had lighted up the heavens that she might win her love. With one glad cry, almost instinctively, she grasped the blossom and fell senseless to the ground. Nor did she stir. Life seemed utterly gone from her frail and slender form. There she lay, a cold, stark figure, while the pelting rain whirled in solid sheets about her, and almost continuous flashes of lightning illumined her pale, wet face with fantastic reds and blues and greens. Yet still she moved not.

ACT V

SCENE 1. THE RITE OF NAKED SWORD

THE sun was slowly rising over a new and beautiful world, washed and refreshed by the night's storm. The little birds woke one by one, and after preening their brilliant plumage, swelled forth a hymn of praise that seemed to say, "All storms will pass and God still lives and loves always." These were the words that again and again repeated themselves in a numb sort of way in Rabiacca's mind until the dulled brain at last seemed to catch and understand them. "All storms will pass and God still lives and loves always."

Painfully she arose from the ground and noted with joy that the mystic herbs were still clasped in her hand, even the last little flower from off the rock. She dried her robe as best she could and sat down to collect her thoughts and remember what had happened during the night.

How calm and peaceful the city looked in the early morning light! The sleepy guards upon the walls were giving place to their relief, and the words of command and the clank of the chain armor floated with startling distinctness through the clear morning air. A few early peasants riding on their diminutive burros were approaching the gates, but still the city slept on in the rising sun like a peacefully sleeping child smiling at its mother's last caress.

Rabiacca hastened to descend the path, for she was anxious to enter, unnoticed, the inner temple gate, where Balixus was to await her and conduct her to the Queen. In his stead, however, she found her foster brother, Mungo, who said he had come to relieve Balixus just before the storm broke, soon after midnight, but he had found the post deserted.

It had been a fearful night, he said. All through the castle had walked the dead. Many of the guards told how they had heard strange voices that were not of earth go whispering through the halls. Some of the priests said they had heard a piercing shriek rise from out the sacred crypt and die away in rolling thunder.

But of course that was but imagined by their fearsome minds; for it was known that the Priestess-Queen herself would pass the night there praying beside the Sacred Fire. Yet there were those who said the Spirits of the Flame were angry, and resented the breaking of the ancient custom whereby the Queen was to escape the Flaming Pyre.

Others declared that all was lost and the nation's glory was at an end, for they had distinctly seen their white Priestess-Queen, who had come from the Land-of-the-Gods, return thither through the air, riding on a thunderbolt, ruling and guiding it with a wand of fire.

Rabiacca pushed aside the garrulous Mungo and quickly descended to the crypt through the priests' passageway. One look, and with a cry of terror, she swooned upon the bottom step. The alarm was quickly sounded, and the passage leading to that chamber of horror was soon crowded with priests and guards. The floor was blotched with pools of blood whose sickly odor, mingled with the half dissipated fumes of the incense, filled the crypt with an almost suffocating smell. The feeble flame still burning on the altar shed a wan half-light upon the drawn and pallid faces of the dead, and only served to increase the ghastly weirdness of that silent scene.

The position of the bodies, and the fact that the Prince's own sword was still protruding from his back, indicated plainly to the assembled officers that the "Rite of Naked Sword" had been performed. But for what reason? It was well known among the priests that since the death of the King, Balixus had been acting as the bodyguard of the Priestess on account of the plotting of those with whom Maldingo was suspected of conspiring to place Zanzibaris on the throne. It was therefore dear that the Queen had met her death through either Maldingo or Zanzibaris, and that in some way Balixus must have forced them to undergo the ancient Rite. All the bodies were cold and stark save alone that of the Priestess. Her flesh was still warm, and she showed some signs of life. Her eyes were open, and, though unseeing, were lit with expression of glad expectancy, and her face appeared radiant with happiness instead of being frozen with horror as might have been expected. The rent in her robe where the sword had pierced was tinged with blood, evidently only by its withdrawal, for no stream of blood had flowed. More marvelous still, the wound seemed already partly healed!

The bodies were removed and a council of the priests and the Twenty Lords was quickly called to consider the awful tragedy. This council had scarce begun its grave deliberations when a commotion was heard at the entrance, and the heavy leathern curtains were suddenly thrust aside and Rabiacca, pale and haggard, her damp hair still streaming in wild disarray over her shoulders, and her bedraggled robe clinging to her girlish form, thrust herself into their august presence despite the detaining hands of the guards. Dropping upon one knee, she raised her arms toward the high priest Votan, who was presiding, and said: "Great Father, I beg thee hear my plea."

"What unseemly haste is this that makest thou, a woman, burst thus upon our solemn council unannounced? Yet seeing thou art so o'erwrought that scarce thy wits can answer for thy act, we give thee clemency and bid thee speak."

"I have sought admission to thy council chamber that I might plead with thee for right to ascend the Flaming Pyre with my dead Lord, Prince Zanzibaris."

"My daughter, thou forgettest that thy lover hath done murder and by the law must be denied the holy purifying flame, and in the pit be slow consumed with gnawing heat from the disintegrating Rock of Thor[*] thrown out."

As though stung by a viper, Rabiacca leaped to her feet, and disregarding all the rules of reverence, cried: "No! No! Great Father! Not the fate of a common felon! He whose veins the royal blood did run! Yes, who since his brother's death, by law, hath been our King! Ah, thou canst not suffer such an end for one whose valor and whose mighty deeds, by the gods themselves inspired, both saved our race and made great our name among all

---

[1] Quick lime.

the earth! And besides, O father, he is my dear loved lord, and I cannot bear this added shame.

Deny me if thou wilt, but let my lord—"

"Peace, my child. Thou asketh much and raiseth grave questions pertaining to the welfare of the state. Perchance our council will consider thine appeal. Thou mayest await without."

At a motion from Votan, Rabiacca was led to an antechamber, a prey to every fear, yet hoping that her prayer would be granted.

SCENE 2. THE FLAMING PYRE AND THE PROPHECY

After much grave discussion, the council decided it would best serve the ends of state, and pacify the followers of the Prince, to allow Zanzibaris to be burned, but without the resinous woods, oils, spices, and fragrant herbs customary for one of his royal rank. Rabiacca was given permission to mount the pyre with him, for although they had not been wed, yet the blood ceremony of betrothal was held almost as sacred as the marriage rite itself, and Rabiacca's great desire to sacrifice herself with her lord, criminal though he was, won for her the unusual privilege. All the ceremonial dances and stately pageantry, however, that would have accompanied the burning of a Prince or King, were to be denied, and only the rites belonging to a warrior of noble birth permitted.

The funeral pyres were arranged for the following evening at sunset. Around that of Zanzibaris, situated apart at some distance from the others, were gathered a great concourse of fighting men and chieftains whom he had led to victory in the many campaigns which he had commanded.

Only a small procession of priests approached the pyre upon which the body of Zanzibaris already lay in state, and in their midst walked Rabiacca. She was clad in a simple flowing robe of white, with her blue-black hair smoothly parted in the middle, falling over her bosom in two large braids decorated with bright grasses and gay, colored feathers. Upon her brow was painted the mark worn by virgins when prepared for the marriage ceremony. She circled with the priests three times around the bier and then ascended to her place upon the pile. As the priests applied the torch below, she placed a farewell kiss upon the lips of the dead Prince and stood erect. As the flames rose higher and higher and began to lick about her naked feet, and scorch her robe, she raised her bracelet-covered arms amid the smoke and shooting tongues of flame and chanted her last farewell. "Ascend, ye sacred flames, and wrap me close! Clasped in thy bright and purifying arms, waft me to heaven with my dear Lord, that I may serve him there and win again, perchance, the love he once did bear for me. Thus without aid of cactus' smoke or burning herb, nor yet of agave's juice, I welcome to my tender flesh Thy piercing darts, and bid them burn away the dross of earthly form that keeps my spirit back from joining my loved lord."

Raised by the strength of her emotions to a divine frenzy, she cried out as if inspired:

"Hear ye my prophecy, O ye priests and men of Tulapan! Our Queen shall come again! She is not dead! Even now she bids me tell thee that the third stone from the altar's top ye will find unloosed, and behind it is a scroll on which is written what ye shall do to keep her earthly form yet living until the time of her return. Seek ye it out and follow well its commands! But the others must with me still follow her into the shades and serve her there through many lives until our task is done. Then will she return to you and bring again her own. So reap we all what we have sown. Zanzibaris!—My queen!—My lord!—Gladly do I come! I come!"